Table of Contents

20 Minutes or Less

15-Minute Chicken & Rice Dinner

    1 tablespoon vegetable oil
    4 skinless, boneless chicken breast halves (about 1 pound)
    1 can (10³/₄ ounces) CAMPBELL'S® Condensed Cream of
        Chicken Soup *or* 98% Fat Free Cream of Chicken Soup
1¹/₂ cups water*
  ¹/₄ teaspoon paprika
  ¹/₄ teaspoon pepper
1¹/₂ cups *uncooked* instant white rice
    2 cups fresh *or* thawed frozen broccoli flowerets

For creamier rice, increase water to 1²/₃ cups.

1. In medium skillet over medium-high heat, heat oil. Add chicken and cook 8 minutes or until browned. Set chicken aside. Pour off fat.

2. Add soup, water, paprika and pepper. Heat to a boil.

3. Stir in rice and broccoli. Place chicken on rice mixture. Season chicken with additional paprika and pepper. Reduce heat to low. Cover and cook 5 minutes or until chicken is no longer pink.

Makes 4 servings

Prep/Cook Time: 15 minutes

Asian Chicken Stir-Fry

1 tablespoon vegetable oil

1 pound skinless, boneless chicken breasts, cut into strips

1 can (10³/₄ ounces) CAMPBELL'S® Condensed Golden
    Mushroom Soup

3 tablespoons soy sauce

1 teaspoon garlic powder

1 bag (16 ounces) any frozen vegetable combination, thawed

4 cups hot cooked rice

1. In medium skillet over medium-high heat, heat oil. Add chicken and stir-fry until browned and juices evaporate.

2. Add soup, soy sauce and garlic powder. Heat to a boil. Reduce heat to medium. Add vegetables and cook until vegetables are tender-crisp, stirring often. Serve over rice.

Makes 4 servings

Prep/Cook Time: 20 minutes

Asian Chicken Stir-Fry

Quick Beef Skillet

> 1 pound ground beef
>
> 1 can (10³/4 ounces) CAMPBELL'S® Condensed Tomato
> Soup
>
> ¹/4 cup water
>
> 1 tablespoon Worcestershire sauce
>
> ¹/4 teaspoon pepper
>
> 1 can (about 15 ounces) sliced potatoes, drained
>
> 1 can (about 8 ounces) sliced carrots, drained

1. In medium skillet over medium-high heat, cook beef until browned, stirring to separate meat. Pour off fat.

2. Add soup, water, Worcestershire, pepper, potatoes and carrots. Reduce heat to low and heat through.

Makes 4 servings

Prep/Cook Time: 15 minutes

Lemon Asparagus Chicken

1 tablespoon vegetable oil

4 skinless, boneless chicken breast halves (about 1 pound)

1 can (10³/₄ ounces) CAMPBELL'S® Condensed Cream of
   Asparagus Soup

¹/₄ cup milk

1 tablespoon lemon juice

¹/₈ teaspoon pepper

1. In medium skillet over medium-high heat, heat oil. Add chicken and cook 8 minutes or until browned. Set chicken aside. Pour off fat.

2. Add soup, milk, lemon juice and pepper. Heat to a boil. Return chicken to pan. Reduce heat to low. Cover and cook 5 minutes or until chicken is no longer pink.

Makes 4 servings

Prep/Cook Time: 20 minutes

Hearty Chicken Noodle Soup

  2 cans (10^1/$_2$ ounces each) CAMPBELL'S® Condensed
    Chicken Broth
  1 cup water
    Generous dash pepper
  1 medium carrot, sliced (about ^{1}/$_2$ cup)
  1 stalk celery, sliced (about ^{1}/$_2$ cup)
  2 skinless, boneless chicken breast halves, cut up
^{1}/$_2$ cup *uncooked* medium egg noodles

1. In medium saucepan mix broth, water, pepper, carrot, celery and chicken. Over medium-high heat, heat to a boil.

2. Stir in noodles. Reduce heat to medium. Cook 10 minutes or until noodles are done, stirring often.

Makes 4 servings

Tip: Save time by using precut carrots and celery from your supermarket salad bar.

Prep/Cook Time: 20 minutes

Easy Beef & Pasta

  1 pound boneless beef sirloin steak, ^{3}/$_4$ inch thick
  1 tablespoon vegetable oil
  1 can (10^3/$_4$ ounces) CAMPBELL'S® Condensed Tomato
    Soup
^{1}/$_2$ cup water
  1 bag (about 16 ounces) frozen side dish seasoned pasta and
    vegetable combination

1. Slice beef into very thin strips.

2. In medium skillet over medium-high heat, heat oil. Add beef and cook until beef is browned and juices evaporate, stirring often.

3. Add soup, water and vegetable combination. Heat to a boil. Reduce heat to low. Cover and cook 5 minutes or until beef and vegetables are done, stirring occasionally.

Makes 4 servings

Tip: For easier slicing, place beef in the freezer for 45 to 60 minutes until it is partially frozen, then cut it into very thin slices.

Prep/Cook Time: 20 minutes

Easy Beef & Pasta

Chicken & Broccoli Alfredo

½ package *uncooked* linguine (8 ounces)
1 cup fresh *or* frozen broccoli flowerets
2 tablespoons butter *or* margarine
1 pound skinless, boneless chicken breasts, cubed
1 can (10¾ ounces) CAMPBELL'S® Condensed Cream of
    Mushroom Soup *or* 98% Fat Free Cream of Mushroom
    Soup
½ cup milk
½ cup grated Parmesan cheese
¼ teaspoon freshly ground pepper

1. Prepare linguine according to package directions. Add broccoli for last 4 minutes of cooking time.

2. In medium skillet over medium-high heat, heat butter. Add chicken and cook until browned, stirring often. Drain.

3. Add soup, milk, cheese, pepper and linguine mixture and cook through, stirring occasionally. Serve with additional Parmesan cheese.

Makes 4 servings

Prep/Cook Time: 20 minutes

Chicken & Broccoli Alfredo

Skillet Meals

Country Skillet Supper

1 pound ground beef

1 medium onion, chopped (about $^1/_2$ cup)

$^1/_8$ teaspoon garlic powder *or* 1 clove garlic, minced

1 can (10$^3/_4$ ounces) CAMPBELL'S® Condensed Golden Mushroom Soup

1 can (10$^1/_2$ ounces) CAMPBELL'S® Condensed Beef Broth

1 can (14$^1/_2$ ounces) diced tomatoes

1 small zucchini, sliced (about 1 cup)

$^1/_2$ teaspoon dried thyme leaves, crushed

1$^1/_2$ cups *uncooked* corkscrew pasta

1. In medium skillet over medium-high heat, cook beef, onion and garlic powder until beef is browned, stirring to separate meat. Pour off fat.

2. Add soup, broth, tomatoes, zucchini and thyme. Heat to a boil. Stir in pasta. Reduce heat to low. Cook 15 minutes or until pasta is done, stirring often.

Makes 4 servings

For a delicious variation, make CAMPBELL'S®
Country Skillet Supper Provençal by topping this
dish with sliced pitted ripe olives.

Lemon Broccoli Chicken

1 lemon

1 tablespoon vegetable oil

4 skinless, boneless chicken breast halves (about 1 pound)

1 can (10¾ ounces) CAMPBELL'S® Condensed Cream of
    Broccoli Soup *or* 98% Fat Free Cream of Broccoli Soup

¼ cup milk

⅛ teaspoon pepper

1. Cut 4 thin slices of lemon and set aside. Squeeze 2 teaspoons juice from remaining lemon and set aside.

2. In medium skillet over medium-high heat, heat oil. Add chicken and cook 10 minutes or until browned. Set chicken aside. Pour off fat.

3. Add soup, milk, reserved lemon juice and pepper. Heat to a boil. Return chicken to pan. Top with lemon slices. Reduce heat to low. Cover and cook 5 minutes or until chicken is no longer pink.

Makes 4 servings

Lemon Broccoli Chicken

Autumn Pork Chops

>   1 tablespoon vegetable oil
>   4 pork chops, ³/₄ inch thick (about 1¹/₂ pounds)
>   1 can (10³/₄ ounces) CAMPBELL'S® Condensed Cream of
>   Celery Soup *or* 98% Fat Free Cream of Celery Soup
>   ¹/₂ cup apple juice *or* water
>   2 tablespoons spicy brown mustard
>   1 tablespoon honey
>   Generous dash pepper

1. In medium skillet over medium-high heat, heat oil. Add chops and cook 10 minutes or until browned. Set chops aside. Pour off fat.

2. Add soup, apple juice, mustard, honey and pepper. Heat to a boil. Return chops to pan. Reduce heat to low. Cover and cook 10 minutes or until chops are no longer pink.

Makes 4 servings

You can store uncooked fresh pork tightly wrapped in
butcher paper in the refrigerator up to four or five days.
Freeze uncooked pork for up to one month.

Honey-Mustard Chicken

1 tablespoon butter *or* margarine

4 skinless, boneless chicken breast halves (about 1 pound)

1 can (10¾ ounces) CAMPBELL'S® Condensed Cream of
    Chicken Soup *or* 98% Fat Free Cream of Chicken Soup

¼ cup mayonnaise

2 tablespoons honey

1 tablespoon spicy brown mustard

Chopped toasted pecans *or* walnuts

1. In medium skillet over medium-high heat, heat butter. Add chicken and cook 10 minutes or until browned. Set chicken aside.

2. Add soup, mayonnaise, honey and mustard. Heat to a boil. Return chicken to pan. Reduce heat to low. Cover and cook 5 minutes or until chicken is no longer pink. Sprinkle with pecans. Serve with rice if desired.

Makes 4 servings

Jambalaya One Dish

1 tablespoon vegetable oil

1/2 pound skinless, boneless chicken breasts, cut up

1/2 pound hot Italian pork sausage, sliced

1/4 teaspoon garlic powder *or* 2 cloves garlic, minced

1 can (10 1/2 ounces) CAMPBELL'S® Condensed French
   Onion Soup

1/3 cup PACE® Picante Sauce *or* Thick & Chunky Salsa

1 cup *uncooked* instant white rice

1/2 cup frozen peas

1/2 pound frozen cooked large shrimp

1. In medium skillet over medium-high heat, heat oil. Add chicken, sausage and garlic powder and cook 5 minutes or until browned, stirring often. Pour off fat.

2. Add soup and picante sauce. Heat to a boil. Stir in rice, peas and shrimp. Reduce heat to low. Cover and cook 5 minutes or until chicken and sausage are no longer pink and most of liquid is absorbed.

Makes 4 servings

Jambalaya One Dish

Easy Chicken & Pasta

    1 tablespoon vegetable oil

    1 pound skinless, boneless chicken breasts, cut up

    1 can (10¾ ounces) CAMPBELL'S® Condensed Cream of
        Mushroom Soup *or* 98% Fat Free Cream of Mushroom
        Soup

2¼ cups water

  ½ teaspoon dried basil leaves, crushed

    2 cups frozen vegetable combination (broccoli, cauliflower,
        carrots)

    2 cups *uncooked* corkscrew macaroni
        Grated Parmesan cheese

1. In medium skillet over medium-high heat, heat oil. Add chicken and cook until browned, stirring often. Set chicken aside.

2. Add soup, water, basil and vegetables. Heat to a boil. Add macaroni. Reduce heat to medium. Cook 10 minutes, stirring often.

3. Return chicken to pan. Cook 5 minutes more or until macaroni is done, stirring often. Sprinkle with cheese.

Makes 4 servings

Easy Chicken & Pasta

Shortcut Stroganoff

   1 pound boneless beef sirloin steak, ³/₄ inch thick
   1 tablespoon vegetable oil
   1 can (10³/₄ ounces) CAMPBELL'S® Condensed Cream of
      Mushroom Soup *or* 98% Fat Free Cream of Mushroom
      Soup
   1 can (10¹/₂ ounces) CAMPBELL'S® Condensed Beef Broth
   1 cup water
   2 teaspoons Worcestershire sauce
   3 cups *uncooked* corkscrew pasta
   ¹/₂ cup sour cream

1. Slice beef into very thin strips.

2. In medium skillet over medium-high heat, heat oil. Add beef and cook until beef is browned and juices evaporate, stirring often.

3. Add soup, broth, water and Worcestershire. Heat to a boil. Stir in pasta. Reduce heat to medium. Cook 15 minutes or until pasta is done, stirring often. Stir in sour cream. Heat through.

Makes 4 servings

Tomato-Basil Chicken

   1 tablespoon vegetable oil
   4 skinless, boneless chicken breast halves (about 1 pound)
   1 can (10³/₄ ounces) CAMPBELL'S® Condensed Tomato
      Soup
   ¹/₂ cup milk
   2 tablespoons grated Parmesan cheese
   ¹/₂ teaspoon dried basil leaves, crushed
   ¹/₄ teaspoon garlic powder *or* 2 cloves garlic, minced
   4 cups hot cooked medium tube-shaped macaroni (about
      3 cups uncooked)

1. In medium skillet over medium-high heat, heat oil. Add chicken and cook 10 minutes or until browned. Set chicken aside. Pour off fat.

2. Add soup, milk, cheese, basil and garlic powder. Heat to a boil. Return chicken to pan. Reduce heat to low. Cover and cook 5 minutes or until chicken is no longer pink. Serve with macaroni.

Makes 4 servings

Tomato-Basil Chicken

Chicken Dijon

Vegetable cooking spray

4 skinless, boneless chicken breast halves (about 1 pound)

1 can (10³/₄ ounces) CAMPBELL'S® Condensed Cream of
   Celery Soup *or* 98% Fat Free Cream of Celery Soup

²/₃ cup water

1 tablespoon Dijon-style mustard

¹/₈ teaspoon pepper

4 cups hot cooked rice

1. Spray medium skillet with cooking spray and heat over medium-high heat 1 minute. Add chicken and cook 10 minutes or until browned. Set chicken aside.

2. Add soup, water, mustard and pepper. Heat to a boil. Return chicken to pan. Reduce heat to low. Cover and cook 5 minutes or until chicken is no longer pink. Serve with rice.

Makes 4 servings

Two-Bean Chili

  1 pound ground beef
  1 large green bell pepper, chopped (about 1 cup)
  1 large onion, chopped (about 1 cup)
  2 tablespoons chili powder
  ¼ teaspoon black pepper
  3 cups CAMPBELL'S® Tomato Juice
  1 can (about 15 ounces) kidney beans, rinsed and drained
  1 can (about 15 ounces) great Northern *or* white kidney
      (cannellini) beans, rinsed and drained
  Sour cream
  Sliced green onions
  Shredded Cheddar cheese
  Chopped tomato

1. In medium skillet over medium-high heat, cook beef, green pepper, onion, chili powder and black pepper until beef is browned, stirring to separate meat. Pour off fat.

2. Add tomato juice and beans and heat through. Top with sour cream, green onions, cheese and tomato.

Makes 6 servings

For a cool refresher, mix ³/₄ cup CAMPBELL'S® Tomato Juice with ¹/₄ cup ginger ale and 1 tablespoon lemon juice. Serve over ice (garnish with a lemon slice.

Beefy Macaroni Skillet

　1　pound ground beef
　1　medium onion, chopped (about $^1/_2$ cup)
　1　can (10$^3/_4$ ounces) CAMPBELL'S® Condensed Tomato
　　　Soup
$^1/_4$　cup water
　1　tablespoon Worcestershire sauce
$^1/_2$　cup shredded Cheddar cheese (2 ounces)
　2　cups cooked corkscrew macaroni (about 1$^1/_2$ cups uncooked)

1. In medium skillet over medium-high heat, cook beef and onion until beef is browned, stirring to separate meat. Pour off fat.

2. Add soup, water, Worcestershire, cheese and macaroni. Reduce heat to low and heat through.

Makes 4 servings

Variation: Substitute 2 cups cooked elbow macaroni (about 1 cup uncooked) for corkscrew macaroni.

This one-skillet family-pleaser works perfectly as
a busy weekday or casual weekend meal.

Beefy Macaroni Skillet

Cajun Fish

1 tablespoon vegetable oil

1 small green pepper, diced (about ²/₃ cup)

¹/₂ teaspoon dried oregano leaves, crushed

1 can (10³/₄ ounces) CAMPBELL'S® Condensed
     Tomato Soup

¹/₃ cup water

¹/₈ teaspoon garlic powder

¹/₈ teaspoon black pepper

¹/₈ teaspoon ground red pepper

1 pound firm white fish fillets (cod, haddock or halibut)

1. In medium skillet over medium heat, heat oil. Add green pepper and oregano and cook until tender-crisp, stirring often. Add soup, water, garlic powder, black pepper and red pepper. Heat to a boil.

2. Place fish in soup mixture. Reduce heat to low. Cover and cook 5 minutes or until fish flakes easily when tested with a fork. Serve with rice, if desired.

Makes 4 servings

Cajun Fish

Skillet Fiesta Chicken & Rice

> 1 tablespoon vegetable oil
> 4 skinless, boneless chicken breast halves (about 1 pound)
> 1 can (10¾ ounces) CAMPBELL'S® Condensed Tomato Soup
> 1⅓ cups water
> 1 teaspoon chili powder
> 1½ cups *uncooked* instant white rice
> ¼ cup shredded Cheddar cheese (1 ounce)

1. In medium skillet over medium-high heat, heat oil. Add chicken and cook 10 minutes or until browned. Set chicken aside. Pour off fat.

2. Add soup, water and chili powder. Heat to a boil.

3. Stir in rice. Place chicken on rice mixture. Sprinkle chicken with additional chili powder and cheese. Reduce heat to low. Cover and cook 5 minutes or until chicken and rice are done. Stir rice mixture.

Makes 4 servings

Always be sure to cook chicken thoroughly, to a minimum internal temperature of 165°F.

Skillet Fiesta Chicken & Rice

Casseroles

Beef Taco Bake

1 pound ground beef

1 can (10¾ ounces) CAMPBELL'S® Condensed Tomato
Soup

1 cup PACE® Thick & Chunky Salsa *or* Picante Sauce

½ cup milk

6 flour tortillas (8-inch) *or* 8 corn tortillas (6-inch), cut into
1-inch pieces

1 cup shredded Cheddar cheese (4 ounces)

1. In medium skillet over medium-high heat, cook beef until browned, stirring to separate meat. Pour off fat.

2. Add soup, salsa, milk, tortillas and **half** the cheese. Spoon into 2-quart shallow baking dish. Cover.

3. Bake at 400°F. for 30 minutes or until hot. Sprinkle with remaining cheese.

Makes 4 servings

Easy Chicken & Biscuits

1 can (10³/₄ ounces) CAMPBELL'S® Condensed Cream of
    Celery Soup *or* 98% Fat Free Cream of Celery Soup

1 can (10³/₄ ounces) CAMPBELL'S® Condensed Cream of
    Potato Soup

1 cup milk

¹/₄ teaspoon dried thyme leaves, crushed

¹/₄ teaspoon pepper

4 cups cooked cut-up vegetables*

2 cups cubed cooked chicken, turkey *or* ham

1 package (7¹/₂ or 10 ounces) refrigerated buttermilk biscuits
    (10 biscuits)

Use a combination of broccoli flowerets, cauliflower flowerets and sliced carrots or broccoli flowerets and sliced carrots or broccoli flowerets, sliced carrots and peas.

1. In 3-quart shallow baking dish mix soups, milk, thyme, pepper, vegetables and chicken.

2. Bake at 400°F. for 15 minutes or until hot.

3. Stir. Arrange biscuits over chicken mixture. Bake 15 minutes more or until biscuits are golden.

Makes 5 servings

*To microwave vegetables, in
2-quart shallow microwave-safe baking
dish arrange vegetables and ¹/₄ cup water.
Cover. Microwave on HIGH 10 minutes.*

Easy Chicken & Biscuits

Baked Macaroni & Cheese

    1 can (10³/₄ ounces) CAMPBELL'S® Condensed Cheddar
        Cheese Soup
    ¹/₂ soup can milk
    ¹/₈ teaspoon pepper
    2 cups hot cooked corkscrew *or* medium shell macaroni
        (about 1¹/₂ cups uncooked)
    1 tablespoon dry bread crumbs
    2 teaspoons margarine *or* butter, melted

1. In 1-quart casserole mix soup, milk, pepper and macaroni.

2. Mix bread crumbs with margarine and sprinkle over macaroni mixture.

3. Bake at 400°F. for 20 minutes or until hot.

Makes 4 servings

Variation: Substitute 2 cups hot cooked elbow macaroni (about 1 cup uncooked) for corkscrew *or* shell macaroni.

To Double Recipe: *Double all ingredients, except increase margarine to 1 tablespoon, use 2-quart casserole and increase baking time to 25 minutes.*

Baked Macaroni & Cheese

One-Dish Chicken & Rice Bake

1 can (10³/4 ounces) CAMPBELL'S® Condensed Cream of Mushroom Soup *or* 98% Fat Free Cream of Mushroom Soup

1 cup water*

³/4 cup *uncooked* regular white rice

¹/4 teaspoon paprika

¹/4 teaspoon pepper

4 skinless, boneless chicken breast halves (about 1 pound)

For creamier rice, increase water to 1¹/3 cups.

1. In 2-quart shallow baking dish mix soup, water, rice, paprika and pepper. Place chicken on rice mixture. Sprinkle with additional paprika and pepper. Cover.

2. Bake at 375°F. for 45 minutes or until chicken is no longer pink and rice is done.

Makes 4 servings

Cod Vera Cruz

1 pound fresh *or* thawed frozen cod *or* haddock fillets

1 can (10¾ ounces) CAMPBELL'S® Condensed Tomato
    Soup

1 can (10½ ounces) CAMPBELL'S® Condensed Chicken
    Broth

⅓ cup PACE® Thick & Chunky Salsa *or* Picante Sauce

1 tablespoon lime juice

2 teaspoons chopped fresh cilantro

1 teaspoon dried oregano leaves, crushed

⅛ teaspoon garlic powder *or* 1 clove garlic, minced

4 cups hot cooked rice

1. Place fish in 2-quart shallow baking dish.

2. Mix soup, broth, salsa, lime juice, cilantro, oregano and garlic
powder. Pour over fish. Bake at 400°F. for 20 minutes or until fish
flakes easily when tested with a fork. Serve over rice.

Makes 4 servings

3-Cheese Pasta Bake

1 can (10¾ ounces) CAMPBELL'S® Condensed Cream of
    Mushroom Soup *or* 98% Fat Free Cream of Mushroom
    Soup

1 package (8 ounces) shredded 2-cheese blend (2 cups)

⅓ cup grated Parmesan cheese

1 cup milk

¼ teaspoon pepper

4 cups cooked corkscrew pasta (about 3 cups uncooked)

In 1½-quart casserole mix soup, cheeses, milk and pepper. Stir in pasta.
Bake at 400°F. for 20 minutes or until hot.

Makes 4 servings

Tuna Noodle Casserole

1 can (10³/₄ ounces) CAMPBELL'S® Condensed Cream of
   Mushroom Soup *or* 98% Fat Free Cream of Mushroom
   Soup

¹/₂ cup milk

2 tablespoons chopped pimiento (optional)

1 cup cooked peas

2 cans (about 6 ounces *each*) tuna, drained and flaked

2 cups hot cooked medium egg noodles (about 1 cup
   uncooked)

2 tablespoons dry bread crumbs

1 tablespoon margarine *or* butter, melted

1. In 1¹/₂-quart casserole mix soup, milk, pimiento, peas, tuna and noodles. Bake at 400°F. for 20 minutes or until hot.

2. Stir. Mix bread crumbs with margarine and sprinkle over noodle mixture. Bake 5 minutes more.

Makes 4 servings

*For a cheesy bread topping, mix ¹/₄ cup shredded
Cheddar cheese (about 1 ounce) with bread crumbs
and margarine. For a change of taste, substitute
1 can (10³/₄ ounces) CAMPBELL'S® Condensed
Cream of Celery Soup **or** 98% Fat Free Cream of
Celery Soup for Cream of Mushroom Soup.*

Tuna Noodle Casserole

King Ranch Chicken Casserole

  1 can (10¾ ounces) CAMPBELL'S® Condensed Cream of
        Mushroom Soup *or* 98% Fat Free Cream of Mushroom
        Soup
 ¾ cup PACE® Picante Sauce
 ¾ cup sour cream
  1 tablespoon chili powder
  2 medium tomatoes, chopped (about 2 cups)
  3 cups cubed cooked chicken *or* turkey
 12 corn tortillas (6-inch), cut into 1-inch pieces
  1 cup shredded Cheddar cheese (4 ounces)
    Green onion for garnish

1. Mix soup, picante sauce, sour cream, chili powder, tomatoes and chicken.

2. In 2-quart shallow baking dish arrange **half** of tortilla pieces. Top with **half** of chicken mixture. Repeat layers. Sprinkle with cheese.

3. Bake at 350°F. for 40 minutes or until hot. Serve with additional picante sauce and sour cream. Garnish with green onion.

Makes 8 servings

King Ranch Chicken Casserole

Chicken Broccoli Divan

    1 pound fresh broccoli, cut into spears, cooked and drained,
          or 1 package (about 10 ounces) frozen broccoli spears,
          cooked and drained
1 1/2 cups cubed cooked chicken *or* turkey
    1 can (10 3/4 ounces) CAMPBELL'S® Condensed Cream
          of Broccoli Soup
  1/3 cup milk
  1/2 cup shredded Cheddar cheese (2 ounces, optional)
    2 tablespoons dry bread crumbs
    1 tablespoon margarine *or* butter, melted

1. In 9-inch pie plate or 2-quart shallow baking dish, arrange broccoli
and chicken. In small bowl, mix soup and milk and pour over broccoli
and chicken.

2. Sprinkle cheese over soup mixture. Mix bread crumbs with
margarine and sprinkle over cheese.

3. Bake at 400°F. for 25 minutes or until hot.

Makes 4 servings

For a lighter version, substitute 1 can
(10 3/4 ounces) CAMPBELL'S® 98% Fat
Free Cream of Broccoli or Cream of Chicken
Soup.

Chicken Broccoli Divan

Country Chicken Casserole

1 can (10¾ ounces) CAMPBELL'S® Condensed Cream of
   Celery Soup *or* 98% Fat Free Cream of Celery Soup

1 can (10¾ ounces) CAMPBELL'S® Condensed Cream of
   Potato Soup

1 cup milk

¼ teaspoon dried thyme leaves, crushed

⅛ teaspoon pepper

4 cups cooked cut-up vegetables*

2 cups cubed cooked chicken *or* turkey

4 cups prepared PEPPERIDGE FARM® Herb Seasoned
   Stuffing

Use a combination of green beans cut into 1-inch pieces and sliced carrots.

1. In 3-quart shallow baking dish mix soups, milk, thyme, pepper,
vegetables and chicken. Spoon stuffing over chicken mixture.

2. Bake at 400°F. for 25 minutes or until hot.

Makes 5 servings

*For prepared stuffing, heat 1¼ cups water and
4 tablespoons margarine **or** butter to a boil. Remove from heat
and add 4 cups PEPPERIDGE FARM® Herb Seasoned
Stuffing. Mix lightly.*

Country Chicken Casserole

Main Dishes

Shortcut Beef Stew

1 tablespoon vegetable oil
1 pound boneless beef sirloin steak, cut into 1-inch cubes
1 can (10¾ ounces) CAMPBELL'S® Condensed Tomato
   Soup
1 can (10¾ ounces) CAMPBELL'S® Condensed French
   Onion Soup
1 tablespoon Worcestershire sauce
1 bag (24 ounces) frozen vegetables for stew (potatoes, carrots,
   celery)

1. In Dutch oven over medium-high heat, heat oil. Add beef and cook until browned, stirring often. Set beef aside.

2. Add soups, Worcestershire and vegetables. Heat to a boil. Return beef to pan. Reduce heat to low. Cover and cook 10 minutes or until vegetables are tender, stirring occasionally.

Makes 4 servings

Flash Roasted Crispy Ranch Chicken

1 can (10¾ ounces) CAMPBELL'S® Condensed Cream of
   Chicken Soup *or* 98% Fat Free Cream of Chicken Soup

½ cup milk

1 envelope (1 ounce) ranch salad dressing mix

4 skinless, boneless chicken breast halves (about 1 pound)

1½ cups finely crushed tortilla chips

2 tablespoons margarine *or* butter, melted

1. In shallow dish mix soup, milk and dressing mix. Reserve 1 cup for sauce.

2. Dip chicken into soup mixture. Coat with tortilla chips.

3. Place chicken on greased baking sheet. Drizzle with margarine. Bake at 400°F. for 20 minutes or until chicken is no longer pink.

4. In small saucepan over medium heat, heat reserved soup mixture to a boil. Serve with chicken.

Makes 4 servings

Flash Roasted Crispy Ranch Chicken

Creamy Chicken & Wild Rice

2 cans (10³/₄ ounces each) CAMPBELL'S® Condensed
Cream of Chicken Soup *or* 98% Fat Free Cream of
Chicken Soup

1¹/₂ cups water

1 package (6 ounces) seasoned long grain and wild rice mix

4 large carrots, thickly sliced (about 3 cups)

8 skinless, boneless chicken breast halves (about 2 pounds)

Slow Cooker Directions

In slow cooker mix soup, water, rice and carrots. Add chicken and turn
to coat. Cover and cook on **low** 7 to 8 hours or until chicken and rice
are done.

Makes 8 servings

Broccoli & Noodles Supreme

3 cups *uncooked* medium egg noodles

2 cups fresh *or* frozen broccoli flowerets

1 can (10³/₄ ounces) CAMPBELL'S® Condensed Cream of
Chicken Soup *or* 98% Fat Free Cream of Chicken Soup

¹/₂ cup sour cream

¹/₃ cup grated Parmesan cheese

¹/₈ teaspoon pepper

In large saucepan prepare noodles according to package directions. Add
broccoli for last 5 minutes of cooking time. Drain. In same pan mix
soup, sour cream, cheese, pepper and noodle mixture. Over medium
heat, heat through, stirring occasionally.

Makes 5 servings

Turkey & Broccoli Alfredo

6 ounces *uncooked* fettuccine

1 cup fresh *or* frozen broccoli flowerets

1 can (10¾ ounces) CAMPBELL'S® Condensed Cream of
Mushroom Soup *or* 98% Fat Free Cream of Mushroom
Soup

½ cup milk

½ cup grated Parmesan cheese

1 cup cubed cooked turkey

¼ teaspoon freshly ground pepper

1. Prepare fettuccine according to package directions. Add broccoli for last 4 minutes of cooking time. Drain.

2. In same pan mix soup, milk, cheese, turkey, pepper and fettuccine mixture and heat through, stirring occasionally.

Makes 4 servings

Variation: Substitute 8 ounces uncooked spaghetti for fettuccine.

Turkey & Broccoli Alfredo

Homestyle Beef Stew

  2 tablespoons all-purpose flour
$1/8$ teaspoon pepper
  1 pound beef for stew, cut into 1-inch cubes
  1 tablespoon vegetable oil
  1 can (10$1/2$ ounces) CAMPBELL'S® Condensed Beef Broth
$1/2$ cup water
$1/2$ teaspoon dried thyme leaves, crushed
  1 bay leaf
  3 medium carrots (about $1/2$ pound), cut into 1-inch pieces
  2 medium potatoes (about $1/2$ pound), cut into quarters

1. Mix flour and pepper. Coat beef with flour mixture.

2. In Dutch oven over medium-high heat, heat oil. Add beef and cook until browned, stirring often. Set beef aside. Pour off fat.

3. Add broth, water, thyme and bay leaf. Heat to a boil. Return beef to pan. Reduce heat to low. Cover and cook 1$1/2$ hours.

4. Add carrots and potatoes. Cover and cook 30 minutes or until beef is fork-tender, stirring occasionally. Discard bay leaf.

Makes 4 servings

Golden Mushroom Pork & Apples

2 cans (10³/4 ounces each) CAMPBELL'S® Condensed
  Golden Mushroom Soup

¹/2 cup water

1 tablespoon brown sugar

1 tablespoon Worcestershire sauce

1 teaspoon dried thyme leaves, crushed

4 large Granny Smith apples, sliced (about 4 cups)

2 large onions, sliced (about 2 cups)

8 boneless pork chops, ³/4 inch thick (about 2 pounds)

Slow Cooker Directions

In slow cooker mix soup, water, brown sugar, Worcestershire and thyme.
Add apples, onions and pork. Cover and cook on **low** 8 to 9 hours or
until pork is tender.

Makes 8 servings

Golden Mushroom Pork & Apples

Country Beef & Vegetables

1 1/2 pounds ground beef
1 can (26 ounces) CAMPBELL'S® Condensed Tomato Soup
1 tablespoon Worcestershire sauce
1 bag (16 ounces) frozen mixed vegetables
6 cups hot cooked rice
Shredded Cheddar cheese

1. In medium skillet over medium-high heat, cook beef until browned, stirring to separate meat. Pour off fat.

2. Add soup, Worcestershire and vegetables. Heat to a boil. Reduce heat to low. Cook 5 minutes or until vegetables are tender. Serve over rice. Top with cheese.

Makes 6 servings

Always cook ground meat thoroughly,
to a minimum temperature of 155°F.

Country Beef & Vegetables

Shortcut Chicken Cordon Bleu

1 tablespoon margarine *or* butter

4 skinless, boneless chicken breast halves (about 1 pound)

1 can (10³/₄ ounces) CAMPBELL'S® Condensed Cream of
    Chicken Soup *or* 98% Fat Free Cream of Chicken Soup

2 tablespoons water

2 tablespoons Chablis *or* other dry white wine

¹/₂ cup shredded Swiss cheese (2 ounces)

¹/₂ cup chopped cooked ham

4 cups hot cooked medium egg noodles (about 3 cups
    uncooked)

1. In medium skillet over medium-high heat, heat margarine. Add chicken and cook 10 minutes or until browned. Set chicken aside.

2. Add soup, water, wine, cheese and ham. Heat to a boil, stirring often. Return chicken to pan. Reduce heat to low. Cover and cook 5 minutes or until chicken is no longer pink, stirring occasionally. Serve with noodles.

Makes 4 servings

*Store uncooked chicken in the coldest part of your
refrigerator for no more than 2 days before cooking.*

Shortcut Chicken Cordon Bleu

Lemon Chicken

2 cans (10³/₄ ounces each) CAMPBELL'S® Condensed
    Cream of Chicken Soup *or* 98% Fat Free Cream of
    Chicken Soup

¹/₂ cup water

¹/₄ cup lemon juice

2 teaspoons Dijon-style mustard

1¹/₂ teaspoons garlic powder

8 large carrots, thickly sliced (about 6 cups)

8 skinless, boneless chicken breast halves (about 2 pounds)

8 cups hot cooked egg noodles

  Grated Parmesan cheese

Slow Cooker Directions

1. In slow cooker mix soup, water, lemon juice, mustard, garlic powder
and carrots. Add chicken and turn to coat. Cover and cook on **low**
7 to 8 hours or until chicken is done.

2. Serve over noodles. Sprinkle with cheese.

Makes 8 servings

Beef & Broccoli

  1 pound boneless beef sirloin *or* top round steak,
     3/4 inch thick
  1 tablespoon vegetable oil
  1 can (10 3/4 ounces) CAMPBELL'S® Condensed Tomato
     Soup
  3 tablespoons soy sauce
  1 tablespoon vinegar
  1 teaspoon garlic powder
  1/4 teaspoon crushed red pepper (optional)
  3 cups fresh *or* thawed frozen broccoli flowerets
  4 cups hot cooked rice

1. Slice beef into very thin strips.

2. In medium skillet over medium-high heat, heat oil. Add beef and stir-fry until browned and juices evaporate.

3. Add soup, soy sauce, vinegar, garlic powder and pepper. Heat to a boil. Reduce heat to medium. Add broccoli and cook until tender-crisp, stirring occasionally. Serve over rice.

Makes 4 servings

Beef & Broccoli

One-Dish Pasta & Vegetables

> 1 1/2 cups *uncooked* corkscrew macaroni
> 2 medium carrots, sliced (about 1 cup)
> 1 cup broccoli flowerets
> 1 can (10 3/4 ounces) CAMPBELL'S® Condensed Cheddar
>   Cheese Soup
> 1/2 cup milk
> 1 tablespoon prepared mustard

1. In large saucepan, prepare macaroni according to package directions. Add carrots and broccoli for last 5 minutes of cooking time. Drain.

2. In same pan mix soup, milk, mustard and macaroni mixture. Over medium heat, heat through, stirring often.

Makes 5 servings

Classic Campbelled Eggs

> 1 can (10 3/4 ounces) CAMPBELL'S® Condensed Cheddar
>   Cheese Soup
> 8 eggs, beaten
>   Dash pepper
> 2 tablespoons margarine *or* butter
>   Chopped fresh parsley for garnish

1. In medium bowl mix soup, eggs and pepper.

2. In medium skillet over low heat, heat margarine. Add egg mixture. As eggs begin to set, stir lightly so uncooked egg mixture flows to bottom. Cook until set but still moist. Garnish with parsley.

Makes 4 servings

One-Dish Pasta & Vegetables

Side Dishes

Green Bean Casserole

    1 can (10³/4 ounces) CAMPBELL'S® Condensed Cream of
           Mushroom Soup *or* 98% Fat Free Cream of Mushroom
           Soup
 ¹/2 cup milk
    1 teaspoon soy sauce
       Dash pepper
    4 cups cooked cut green beans*
    1 can (2.8 ounces) French's® French Fried Onions (1¹/3 cups)

Use 1 bag (16 to 20 ounces) frozen green beans, 2 packages (9 ounces each) frozen green beans, 2 cans (about 16 ounces each) green beans or about 1¹/2 pounds fresh green beans for this recipe.

1. In 1¹/2-quart casserole mix soup, milk, soy sauce, pepper, beans and ¹/2 **can** onions.

2. Bake at 350°F. for 25 minutes or until hot.

3. Stir. Sprinkle remaining onions over bean mixture. Bake 5 minutes more or until onions are golden.

Makes 6 servings

My anvil rings
  From morn till night.
Good Campbell's Soups
Give me my might!

Cheesy Picante Potatoes

- 1 can (10³/₄ ounces) CAMPBELL'S® Condensed Cheddar Cheese Soup
- ¹/₂ cup PACE® Picante Sauce *or* Thick & Chunky Salsa
- 1 teaspoon garlic powder
- 4 cups cubed cooked potatoes (about 4 medium)
  Paprika
- 2 tablespoons chopped fresh cilantro

In medium skillet mix soup, picante sauce and garlic powder. Add potatoes. Over medium heat, heat through, stirring often. Sprinkle with paprika and cilantro. Serve with additional picante sauce.

Makes 6 to 8 servings

The wallop in my punches
And the hustle in my feet
Are there because of Campbell's,
Which I dearly love to eat.

Cheesy Broccoli

1 can (10¾ ounces) CAMPBELL'S® Condensed Cheddar
    Cheese Soup
¼ cup milk
4 cups frozen broccoli cuts

Microwave Directions

1. In 2-quart microwave-safe casserole, mix soup and milk. Add broccoli.

2. Cover and microwave on HIGH 8 minutes or until broccoli is tender-crisp, stirring once during heating.

Makes 4 servings

Cheesy Broccoli

Scalloped Potato-Onion Bake

1 can (10³/4 ounces) CAMPBELL'S® Condensed Cream of
    Celery Soup *or* 98% Fat Free Cream of Celery Soup

¹/2 cup milk

    Dash pepper

4 medium potatoes (about 1¹/4 pounds), thinly sliced

1 small onion, thinly sliced (about ¹/4 cup)

1 tablespoon margarine *or* butter

    Paprika

1. Mix soup, milk and pepper. In 1¹/2-quart casserole layer **half** of potatoes, onion and soup mixture. Repeat layers. Dot with margarine. Sprinkle with paprika.

2. Cover and bake at 400°F. for 1 hour. Uncover and bake 15 minutes more or until potatoes are tender.

Makes 6 servings

For a variation and dash of color, add
¹/4 cup chopped fresh parsley in step 1.

Creamy Vegetable Medley

    1 can (10¾ ounces) CAMPBELL'S® Condensed Cream of
        Celery Soup *or* 98% Fat Free Cream of Celery Soup
 ½ cup milk
    2 cups broccoli flowerets
    2 medium carrots, sliced (about 1 cup)
    1 cup cauliflower flowerets

1. In medium saucepan mix soup, milk, broccoli, carrots and cauliflower. Over medium heat, heat to a boil.

2. Reduce heat to low. Cover and cook 15 minutes or until vegetables are tender, stirring occasionally.

Makes 6 servings

Variation: Omit milk. Substitute 1 bag (16 ounces) frozen vegetable combination (broccoli, cauliflower, carrots) for fresh vegetables.

71

Cheddary Pouch Potatoes

> 1 can (10¾ ounces) CAMPBELL'S® Condensed Cheddar
>   Cheese Soup
> ¼ cup milk
> ½ teaspoon garlic powder
> ¼ teaspoon onion powder
> 4 cups frozen steak fries
>   Paprika

1. In large bowl mix soup, milk, garlic powder and onion powder. Stir in potatoes.

2. Cut four 14-inch squares of heavy-duty aluminum foil. Spoon **1 cup** soup mixture onto each square, arranging potatoes to make single layer. Sprinkle with paprika. Bring up sides of foil and double fold. Double fold ends to make packet.

3. Place potato packets on grill rack over medium-hot coals. Grill 25 minutes or until potatoes are tender.

Makes 4 servings

Cheddary Oven Pouch Potatoes: In Step 3, on baking sheet bake packets at 350°F. for 25 minutes.

Cheddary Pouch Potatoes

Saucy Asparagus

1 can (10³/4 ounces) CAMPBELL'S® Condensed Cream of
   Asparagus Soup

2 tablespoons milk

1¹/2 pounds asparagus, trimmed, cut into 1-inch pieces (about
   3 cups) *or* 2 packages (10 ounces each) frozen asparagus
   cuts

1. In medium saucepan, mix soup and milk. Over medium heat, heat to
a boil, stirring occasionally.

2. Add asparagus. Reduce heat to low. Cover and cook 10 minutes or
until asparagus is tender, stirring occasionally.

Makes 6 servings

Saucy Asparagus

Cheddar Mashed Potato Bake

1 can (10¾ ounces) CAMPBELL'S® Condensed Cheddar
   Cheese Soup
⅓ cup sour cream *or* plain yogurt
   Generous dash pepper
1 green onion, chopped (about 2 tablespoons)
3 cups stiff, seasoned mashed potatoes

1. In 1½-quart casserole mix soup, sour cream, pepper and onion. Stir in potatoes.

2. Bake at 350°F. for 30 minutes or until hot.

Makes 8 servings

Variation: In small bowl mix 1 tablespoon melted margarine *or* butter, 2 tablespoons dry bread crumbs and ¼ teaspoon paprika. Sprinkle over potato mixture before baking.

To make 3 cups stiff, seasoned mashed potatoes, in medium saucepan place 2 pounds potatoes, peeled and cut into 1-inch pieces. Cover with water. Add salt, if desired. Over high heat, heat to a boil. Reduce heat to medium. Cover and cook 10 minutes or until potatoes are tender. Drain. Mash potatoes with ¾ cup milk and 2 tablespoons margarine or butter. Season to taste with salt and pepper.

Quick Lemon-Broccoli Rice

1 can (10½ ounces) CAMPBELL'S® Condensed Chicken
   Broth

1 cup small broccoli flowerets

1 small carrot, shredded (about ⅓ cup)

1¼ cups *uncooked* instant white rice

2 teaspoons lemon juice

   Generous dash pepper

1. In medium saucepan over high heat, heat broth to a boil. Add broccoli and carrot. Reduce heat to low. Cover and cook 5 minutes or until vegetables are tender.

2. Stir in rice, lemon juice and pepper. Cover and remove from heat. Let stand 5 minutes. Fluff with fork.

Makes 4 servings

Broth Simmered Rice

1 can (10½ ounces) CAMPBELL'S® Condensed Chicken
   Broth
¾ cup water
2 cups *uncooked* instant white rice

In medium saucepan over medium-high heat, heat broth and water to a
boil. Stir in rice. Cover and remove from heat. Let stand 5 minutes.
Fluff with fork.

Makes 4 servings

Cheese Fries

1 bag (32 ounces) frozen French fried potatoes
1 can (10¾ ounces) CAMPBELL'S® Condensed Cheddar
   Cheese Soup

1. On baking sheet, bake potatoes according to package directions.

2. Push potatoes into pile in center of baking sheet. Stir soup in can
and spoon over potatoes.

3. Bake 3 minutes more or until soup is hot.

Makes 6 servings

Nacho Cheese Fries: Substitute CAMPBELL'S® Condensed Fiesta
Nacho Cheese Soup for the Cheddar Cheese Soup.

Cheese Fries

Snacks & Mini-Meals

5-Minute Burrito Wraps

　　1　can (11¼ ounces) CAMPBELL'S® Condensed Fiesta Chili
　　　　　Beef Soup
　　6　flour tortillas (8-inch)
　　　　Shredded Cheddar cheese

Microwave Directions

1. Spoon 2 tablespoons soup down center of each tortilla. Top with cheese. Fold tortilla around filling.

2. Place seam-side down on microwave-safe plate and microwave on HIGH 2 minutes or until hot.

Makes 6 burritos

"WE'RE HAVING OUR FAVORITE SOUP OFTEN THESE DAYS!"

Sloppy Joe Pizza

¾ pound ground beef

1 can (10¾ ounces) CAMPBELL'S® Condensed
     Tomato Soup

1 Italian bread shell (12-inch)

1½ cups shredded Cheddar cheese (6 ounces)

1. In medium skillet over medium-high heat, cook beef until browned, stirring to separate meat. Pour off fat.

2. Add soup. Heat through. Spread beef mixture over shell to within ¼ inch of edge. Top with cheese. Bake at 450°F. for 12 minutes or until cheese is melted.

Makes 4 servings

Cheesesteak Pockets

- 1 **tablespoon vegetable oil**
- 1 **medium onion, sliced (about ¹/2 cup)**
- 1 **package (14 ounces) frozen beef *or* chicken sandwich steaks,
    cut into 8 pieces**
- 1 **can (10³/4 ounces) CAMPBELL'S® Condensed Cheddar
    Cheese Soup**
- 1 **jar (about 4¹/2 ounces) sliced mushrooms, drained**
- 4 **pita breads (6-inch), cut in half, forming two pockets each**

1. In medium skillet over medium-high heat, heat oil. Add onion and cook until tender. Add sandwich steaks and cook 5 minutes or until browned, stirring often. Pour off fat.

2. Add soup and mushrooms. Heat to a boil. Reduce heat to low and heat through. Spoon meat mixture into pita halves.

Makes 4 sandwiches

Cheesesteak Pockets

Cheesy Broccoli Potato Topper

> 1 can (10³/4 ounces) CAMPBELL'S® Condensed Cheddar
>   Cheese Soup
> 4 large hot baked potatoes, split
> 1 cup cooked broccoli flowerets

Microwave Directions

1. Stir soup in can until soup is smooth.

2. Place hot baked potatoes on microwave-safe plate. Carefully fluff up potatoes with fork.

3. Top each potato with broccoli. Spoon soup over potatoes. Microwave on HIGH 4 minutes or until hot.

Makes 4 servings

Shrimp Dip

    1 package (8 ounces) cream cheese, softened

    1 can ($10^3/4$ ounces) CAMPBELL'S® Condensed Cream of
           Shrimp Soup

   $1/2$ teaspoon Louisiana-style hot sauce

   $1/4$ cup finely chopped celery

    1 tablespoon finely chopped onion

Stir cream cheese until smooth. Stir in soup, hot sauce, celery and onion. Refrigerate at least 4 hours. Serve with crackers, chips or fresh vegetables for dipping.

Makes $2^1/4$ cups

Shrimp Dip

Tomato Soup Spice Cake

  1 **package (about 18 ounces) spice cake mix**
  1 **can (10³/₄ ounces) CAMPBELL'S® Condensed Tomato
     Soup**
¹/₂ **cup water**
  2 **eggs**
    Cream Cheese Frosting (recipe follows)

1. Preheat oven to 350°F. Grease and lightly flour two 8- or 9-inch round cake pans.

2. In large bowl mix cake mix, soup, water and eggs according to package directions.

3. Pour into prepared pans. Bake 25 minutes or until toothpick inserted in center comes out clean.

4. Cool on wire racks 10 minutes. Remove from pans and cool completely on wire racks.

5. Fill and frost with Cream Cheese Frosting.

Makes 12 servings

Cream Cheese Frosting: Beat 2 packages (3 ounces *each*) softened cream cheese until smooth. Gradually blend in 1 package (1 pound) sifted confectioners' sugar and ¹/₂ teaspoon vanilla extract. If desired, thin with milk.

Tomato Soup Spice Cake

Quick Beef 'n' Beans Tacos

1 pound ground beef

1 small onion, chopped (about ¼ cup)

1 can (11¼ ounces) CAMPBELL'S® Condensed Fiesta Chili
    Beef Soup

¼ cup water

10 taco shells
    Shredded Cheddar cheese, shredded lettuce, diced tomato
        and sour cream

1. In medium skillet over medium-high heat, cook beef and onion until beef is browned, stirring to separate meat. Pour off fat.

2. Add soup and water. Reduce heat to low. Cover and cook 5 minutes.

3. Divide meat mixture among taco shells. Top with cheese, lettuce, tomato and sour cream.

Makes 10 tacos

Mushroom Mozzarella Bruschetta

1 loaf (about 1 pound) Italian bread (16 inches long), cut in half lengthwise

1 can (10³/₄ ounces) CAMPBELL'S® Condensed Cream of Mushroom Soup *or* 98% Fat Free Cream of Mushroom Soup

¹/₄ teaspoon garlic powder

¹/₄ teaspoon dried Italian seasoning, crushed

1 cup shredded mozzarella cheese (4 ounces)

1 tablespoon grated Parmesan cheese

1 small red pepper, chopped (about ¹/₂ cup)

2 green onions, chopped (about ¹/₄ cup)

1. Bake bread on baking sheet at 400°F. for 5 minutes or until lightly toasted.

2. Mix soup, garlic powder and Italian seasoning. Stir in mozzarella cheese, Parmesan cheese, pepper and onions.

3. Spread soup mixture on bread. Bake 5 minutes or until cheese is melted. Cut each bread half into 4 pieces.

Makes 8 servings

For convenience, use packaged pre-shredded mozzarella cheese. Half an 8-ounce package will provide the 1 cup needed for this recipe.

Nacho Chicken & Rice Wraps

2 cans (10³/4 ounces each) CAMPBELL'S® Condensed
Cheddar Cheese Soup

1 cup water

2 cups PACE® Thick & Chunky Salsa *or* Picante Sauce

1¹/4 cups *uncooked* regular long-grain white rice

2 pounds skinless, boneless chicken breasts, cut into cubes

10 flour tortillas (10-inch)

Slow Cooker Directions

1. In slow cooker mix soup, water, salsa, rice and chicken. Cover and cook on **low** 7 to 8 hours or until chicken and rice are done.

2. Spoon **about 1 cup** rice mixture down center of each tortilla.

3. Fold opposite sides of tortilla over filling. Roll up from bottom. Cut each wrap in half.

Makes 10 servings

For firmer rice, substitute converted rice for regular.

Souperburger Sandwiches

  1 pound ground beef
  1 medium onion, chopped (about ¹/₂ cup)
  1 can (10³/₄ ounces) CAMPBELL'S® Condensed Cheddar
      Cheese Soup
  1 tablespoon prepared mustard
¹/₈ teaspoon pepper
  6 hamburger rolls, split and toasted

1. In medium skillet over medium-high heat, cook beef and onion until beef is browned, stirring to separate meat. Pour off fat.

2. Add soup, mustard and pepper. Reduce heat to low and heat through. Divide meat mixture among rolls.

Makes 6 sandwiches

Nacho Tacos

     1 pound ground beef
     1 medium onion, chopped (about ¹/₂ cup)
  ¹/₂ teaspoon chili powder
     1 can (11 ounces) CAMPBELL'S® Condensed Fiesta Nacho
         Cheese Soup
     8 taco shells
     1 cup shredded lettuce
     1 medium tomato, chopped (about 1 cup)

1. In medium skillet over medium-high heat, cook beef, onion and chili powder until beef is browned, stirring to separate meat. Pour off fat.

2. Add ¹/₂ **cup** soup and heat through.

3. In small saucepan over low heat, heat remaining soup until hot. Divide meat mixture among taco shells. Top with 1¹/₂ **tablespoons** hot soup, lettuce and tomato.

Makes 8 tacos

Pan Roasted Vegetable & Chicken Pizza

Vegetable cooking spray
3/4 pound skinless, boneless chicken breasts, cubed
3 cups cut-up vegetables*
1/8 teaspoon garlic powder *or* 1 clove garlic, minced
1 can (10 3/4 ounces) CAMPBELL'S® Condensed Cream of Mushroom Soup *or* 98% Fat Free Cream of Mushroom Soup
1 Italian bread shell (12-inch)
1 cup shredded Monterey Jack cheese (4 ounces)

*Use a combination of sliced zucchini, red or green pepper cut into 2-inch long strips, and thinly sliced onion.

1. Spray medium skillet with vegetable cooking spray and heat over medium-high heat 1 minute. Add chicken and cook 10 minutes or until browned, stirring often. Set chicken aside.

2. Remove pan from heat. Spray with cooking spray. Reduce heat to medium. Add vegetables and garlic powder. Cook until tender-crisp. Add soup. Return chicken to pan. Heat through.

3. Spread chicken mixture over shell to within 1/4 inch of edge. Top with cheese. Bake at 450°F. for 12 minutes or until cheese is melted.

Makes 4 servings

French Onion Burgers

1 pound ground beef

1 can (10¹/₂ ounces) CAMPBELL'S® Condensed French
   Onion Soup

4 slices cheese (use your favorite)

4 round hard rolls, split

1. Shape beef into 4 patties, ¹/₂ inch thick.

2. In medium skillet over medium-high heat, cook patties until browned. Set patties aside. Pour off fat.

3. Add soup. Heat to a boil. Return patties to pan. Reduce heat to low. Cover and cook 10 minutes or until patties are no longer pink (160°F.).

4. Place cheese on patties and cook until cheese is melted. Place patties on 4 roll halves. Serve with soup mixture for dipping.

Makes 4 sandwiches

French Onion Burger

Buffalo-Style Burgers

 1 pound ground beef
 1 can (10³/₄ ounces) CAMPBELL'S® Condensed Tomato
    Soup
 ¹/₈ teaspoon hot pepper sauce
 4 hamburger rolls, split and toasted
 ¹/₂ cup crumbled blue cheese (about 4 ounces)

1. Shape beef into 4 patties, ¹/₂ inch thick.

2. In medium skillet over medium-high heat, cook patties until browned. Set patties aside. Pour off fat.

3. Add soup and hot pepper sauce. Heat to a boil. Return patties to pan. Reduce heat to low. Cover and cook 10 minutes or until patties are no longer pink (160°F.).

4. Place patties on 4 roll halves. Top with cheese and remaining roll halves.

Makes 4 sandwiches

Buffalo-Style Burger

Index

Fish

INDEX